RIVERAIN

RIVERAIN

James Haug

Oberlin College Press
Oberlin, Ohio

The FIELD Poetry Series, vol. 39
Oberlin College Press, 50 N. Professor Street, Oberlin, OH 44074
www.oberlin.edu/ocpress

Cover and book design: Steve Farkas.
Cover image: Dorothy Lathrop, Final illustration for *Presents for Lupe*
(Macmillan, 1940). Collection of The Eric Carle Museum of Picture Book
Art. Gift of Kendra and Allan Daniel in honor of Nick Clark.

Library of Congress Cataloging-in-Publication Data

Names: Haug, James, 1954- author.
Title: Riverain / James Haug.
Description: Oberlin, Ohio : Oberlin College Press, [2018] | Series: The
    FIELD poetry series ; vol. 39
Identifiers: LCCN 2017053293| ISBN 9780997335521 (paperback : alk. paper) |
    ISBN 0997335521 (paperback : alk. paper)
Classification: LCC PS3558.A75644 A6 2018 | DDC 811/.54--dc23
LC record available at https://lccn.loc.gov/2017053293

for Alix

Contents

I donned at once my *traveling coat*...

—Xavier de Maistre
(trans. Stephen Sartarelli)

A Spot by the River

There was a spot by the river that had nothing in it. It was a perfect spot for a hotel. But everyone had ideas about what kind of hotel it should be. A transient hotel, said the crows. Hotels are by definition transient, said the squirrels. You come, and when it's time, you go. Every good hotel however must have a revolving door. A hotel should feature a good view of the street from every room, the cows said. It's important to spy on who's coming and who's going. A good old-fashioned hotel, said the bears, where a fellow can take up for months at a time, with parties and women, and Do Not Disturb signs. A hotel with a good restaurant, and no questions asked, said the bobcats. And valet parking, the ducks said. Make that underground parking, said the skunks, and a casino. It must be for the whole family, said the badgers. There has to be a chapel, the field mice said, and multi-denominational services. A hotel with rooms by the hour, the trout said, and a pale clerk with yellow teeth working the desk all night, and a mop in a bucket in the hall, and cheap red bibles. The walls must be thin, the frogs said, so you won't forget you're surrounded by others. The walls must be thick, said the wrens, so you won't forget you're all alone. Rooms full of mirrors, said the possums, and access to ledges. Rooms that fit only a bed and an ashtray, the garter snakes said. Rooms that are suites that open into more suites, said the porcupines, and wind billowing the curtains, and monogrammed bathrobes. There should be famous books for children about the hotel, the deer said, with pictures. It should have no sign in front, said the moles. It should have no address, said the owls. It should be built on nothing, the raccoons said, and disappear when you look for it. And hats will be forbidden, said a pair of ferrets, who formed the smallest contingent of all.

Ian's House

The bouncer at Ian's house has it easy. The people who come to Ian's house are the people you expect, people who listen to a little song in their heads, who wear navy wool caps and give secret nods and are inwardly shocked when they see themselves in a mirror. They look high and low for Ian, without urgency. It would be nice to find Ian. If Ian were to appear it would be like a bell ringing in a foyer. If Ian were to appear it would be in the kitchen and he's seated on the counter with a glass of milk in his hand or a dark fabulous cigarette. Nobody ever sees more than half of Ian at a time. He's like a scrap of paper rustling in the corner. He's like a passport picture and goes backwards up the stairs. There are bunk beds and a skylight and a beanpole in Ian's house. The people who come to Ian's house leave Ian's house when it's time to leave, or maybe later. Most nights are quiet nights. Ian's house doesn't need a bouncer. That's what attracted the bouncer to Ian's house.

Fitful Bouts of Dozing

It was the end of the day all day. Looks like London, we said. Not as dark, said the youngest. We woke cloaked in a shroud of mist, and proceeded shrouded in a cloak of fog. It was the end of our beliefs, the beginning of our wanderings. In Iceland it was the middle of the day half the year. That's what we told ourselves later. An unusually high consumption of fish makes Icelanders fairly chipper. They capered among the jagged edges of the landscape, a sleepless frolicsome bunch. We flew over the North Sea at night though it was never fully night. Through our window we saw the earth's curve. The youngest gazed silently down. In Louisiana at night, a faint breeze pressed against the mosquito netting. Let's pretend we're in a jungle, we said, between fitful bouts of dozing. And monkeys are wrestling in the trees, the youngest said. Dense clouds broke sometime after midnight, and a full moon shone a light into our quarters. And then a mockingbird sang, convinced it was day dawning, and we were convinced as well. Like Kansas with the top down, said the youngest.

The River at Dawn

She went for a walk along the river at dawn because a walk along the river at dawn is just the thing. A runner was out with his dog. She could hear them each panting from a long way off because sound carries so well at dawn. There is nothing at dawn to get in the way of sound. Sound is let off its leash at dawn, like a dog running ahead of its person. The other sounds that stop sound, gearboxes and back-up bells and dumpsters, the other sounds that make sound sit down and wait, those sounds have not yet coalesced into a pack of sound. Sound at dawn plays in the dormant yards those other sounds have yet to occupy. Even the river at dawn, a purveyor of sound, makes no sound, so that sound may pass unimpeded across it, a sound of wings, of people running.

Cows Are a Good Idea

All I had to do was cross the next hill, a long low grade with a few far-off trees at the top and a small farmhouse. A woman outside the farmhouse was battling linen billowing in the wind from a clothesline, punching sheets with one hand to make them submit while unclipping clothespins with the other. All I had to do was climb the hill and the day would be over. The sky was brooding above the woman and the laundry, and above some cows. Cows are a good idea, I thought. So are horses, and a vacant drive-in. A few more buildings were coming into view—another farmhouse with laundry, a water tower, a bottling plant. Wind was troubling the awning of a shoe store in a town that emerged where a town should be. A boy with an ice cream cone lost his baseball cap. The road out of town acquired extra lanes. A wide treeless vista spread out in all directions. It was a longer hill than I first thought, which I had in fact been descending all along. Lights of distant towns glittered like effigies of distant towns.

Travel

A box full of things squares itself in a corner. Shows it could be opened. Dusty lid latched by hook & eye. Box without the house it comes with. Box placed squat in the middle of a field. It's June with the box squat in a field with a hole in the ground next to it bigger than a box. In the box it's winter. In it it's after midnight. The box is empty of nightclothes. In the box a cloud expands. Nightclothes spread on the grass. The box is not the only house in a field. The necessity of the field disagrees with the necessity of the box. The box without a house is a box filled of things meant to fill another box. The empty box fills with that for which the box was not made.

First It Didn't Sound Like

First it didn't sound like anything. Then it sounded like someone old getting slowly out of bed but the bed was very far away. Then it sounded like someone upstairs arranging linen in a closet in a 19th-century house. The linen had been flapping in the wind and sun all day. It was tired but refreshed linen from a time of wholesome sleep patterns. Then it sounded like someone across the street dumping charcoal briquettes into an outdoor grill, and a twin-prop cargo plane was passing overhead, and one after one the wooden matches wouldn't light. Then it sounded like someone had discovered an old duffel bag in the attic, and on the duffel bag was a name in stenciled black letters, a name of someone's best friend who no one knows anymore. Then it sounded like someone was pulling a heavy wooden rowboat from a lake one evening in the Adirondacks. It was getting dragged up the shore until it was fully out of the water and the one dragging it fell back to finish a cigarette because it was still summer. Then it sounded like someone having an argument, a parent and a teenager next door, but then it sounded like they were remembering something funny and they were setting dishes on the table. Then it sounded like someone who had found where the mice were getting in, in the basement, but then the light bulb blew out and it sounded like someone trying to get out of the dark. Then it sounded like someone finding the stairs and taking each step carefully, someone who as a kid had kept a dog in the basement one night, when it wasn't okay to keep a dog in the house. Then it sounded like someone lifting something very heavy, and then more people joining in to lift, lifting something heavy and broken like a garage door, and then it sounded like they'd finished and daylight was coming in where the door had been.

In the Woods

There was an afternoon when coming out of the woods was like coming out of the afternoon. And to find oneself in the woods was like finding oneself in a rainstorm. The abandoned house in the woods was a house from a book, a house abandoned in a book, and it was a book about being lost when it rains and finding the house when you need it most, and the house is sweetly furnished with lace curtains and embroidered runners and framed pictures on the walls of cottages situated sweetly in the woods. The book was a book abandoned in a house about being a book in an abandoned house, a book committed to an unreadable tale of flight, of rain in the afternoon, rain in the woods that made the afternoon like twilight in the woods. The house was playing house as we played house inside it and the rain made all of it close and gave us something to wait for. There would be more rain, more woodland to tramp through, our jackets pulled up over our heads. Before the woman who once lived there returned, there was only us to wonder, and since running off, we didn't turn around, we didn't leave a trail.

Dismal Levels

The river was collecting snow on itself. Almost nobody was coming to see it. Its banks were either slick and muddy, or frozen and rutted. The river was letting itself go. Here and there it was jammed with branches that trapped chunks of ice from the current, and plastic jugs and scraps of chicken wire, and there it was that snow collected. Once a day, someone with spikes on his shoes puffed along one of the banks, adding to the available store of good health, another rugged jerk. Oh dismal levels, thought the river, when it came to the subject of water lines. I'm only a murky reflection of the heavens, of winter clouds congealing, broken lines of geese, stars and moon and satellites. The river thought long and hard about what going down to the river must mean. It was the best place, thought the river, to think long and hard.

Maryann's Mad

Maryann's mad about something. All we can do is take a step back. It's we who've supported her this far, bringing her water when she needs it. According to Maryann, Maryann isn't mad. She's washing and drying the dishes and looking out the window, only it's the same dish she keeps washing and drying. The dish is clean by now but no one wants to be the one to tell her. It's better to believe the dish is dirty, and the dish is a thousand dishes, each one dirtier than the next, and that each requires the furious care only Maryann can bring to it. If we could only pitch in, and dive up to our elbows, and worry the dishes with wiping, and stack them in crooked towers just in time for Thanksgiving, if only we could fix things…. We can't say this to Maryann, but Maryann knows the goodness of our intentions. We're here to help, Maryann, lined up outside the kitchen and down the hall, out the front door and down the street. All we can do is what we do. We say we for convenience. What we mean is: I; as in: I am a ghost at large in the invisible neighborhood of Maryann.

Far Away

You can't play a sad song on a banjo. You can play a lullaby or a sonata. You can play a scary song on a banjo. You can fill a room. You can't build a room with a banjo. The banjo itself is the most improbable of designs. Grown men are generally between 1½ and 2½ banjos tall. You can pretend a banjo is a canoe paddle. You can pretend a canoe paddle is a banjo. You can cross a lake, your paddle strumming the water. You can hear a banjo from the shore, a banjo lit by a campfire, a banjo that rattles like a collection plate. The banjo you remember well will sound always far away. Chester A. Arthur is the only president ever photographed with a banjo. In the photograph he's reluctant to touch it. Arthur was unsure what a banjo would do to his already sketchy reputation.

The Turkey Ideal

The wind has gotten under the porch rug, wearing it like a buffalo skin. A jazz album goes flying down the street. It's not my job to catch it. I've had so many jobs. I worked in a car wash and ate nothing but hash brownies, and very often hit a bump in the road. I painted houses, with or without permission. Somehow I got older and drove cabs. My job yesterday was to drive through the town of Hadley. I stopped for four turkeys crossing the road single-file. The safety of the four turkeys was my job. I sat in my cab in the middle of the road and flashed the headlights at oncoming cars to warn them. The turkeys cared nothing about me. I was invisible to them, and that was right. My invisibility to turkeys has long been another of my jobs. I stood still, as per the requirements of employment, I gave wide berth to their passage into the turkey fields, which is their calling. They were the embodiment of the turkey ideal. And I was there to thank them, and flash my lights, as porch furniture went bouncing across our lawns in the great winds that sweep the future toward us. My job now is to be wind-blown. I drive directly below a bald eagle along the road that ends at the river. I'm keeping track of the eagle through the moon roof. I'm listening to my haircut rearrange itself in the wind.

Windmills Minutely Visible

Out the window one morning she saw a giant smokestack by itself in a pasture. Cows were milling around it—black and white cows, handsome next to the enormous gray of the smokestack. No smoke issued from the stack. In fact, it looked cold, the color of old ice among trees and green rolling hills, among parrots and cockatoos, students in sandals, and a vendor selling falafel. She was, she reasoned, not entirely accurate when she called what she saw from her window a pasture. It was more like a small city in Spain, with grass and buildings, where cows could wander and the food was international. Delivery boys rode by on bicycles. A young woman was reading a book. The stack was more like a chimney, and probably older than everything else around it, older even than windmills minutely visible on the horizon. And there was a gas station nearby, with a single pump, and music coming out of the door. Standing inside was her old friend, Oscar, whistling along, and counting the cash.

Off Federal

The river runs behind the house, sleepy in August. People fear it at night. No one's sure what the river's up to. If a river runs beneath a house it gives the house a sense of buried machinery. The river doesn't exist without us. Without the river we don't know where we are. I say we because I approached it once at night in the company of someone else. It was darker than expected. We picked our way slowly. We kept moving and that's what I can tell you.

Tractor in Repose

Yellow leaves skidded across the road in front of Alice's car. Dark pumpkins at the farm stand. Alice had made a thousand phone calls, all in one day alone. She'd be happy not to speak again. For the last hour her hands tingled, an ant-like crawling originating from the palms. She gripped the wheel hard to squash the sensation but it came back stronger once her grip relaxed. Some young black cows from a small dairy farm up ahead were grazing near the roadside. This was better. With no one behind her, Alice eased off the gas. This was good. But then she sensed smoke outside, smoke that had entered the car. She saw no sign of it, no smoke in the trees, no houses burning, but something going wrong. Alice pulled over and left the car. She followed where she thought the smoke was coming from. But she found no evidence. A gray clapboard farmhouse up ahead made no smoke from its chimney, and had no light in the windows. The fields were dry and shade-streaked and not burning. A tractor sat in repose, anchoring its shadow. Alice looked back at the cows sweetly grazing and returned to her car. There was nothing to be done. She couldn't see what it was that needed saving. The bridge rose ahead, traffic midway stalled above the river. She detected smoke every place, the water below flat and cloudy, with a single boat.

Clamor in a Distant Steeple

The rain starts up quickly and quickly stops. Some people are plainly comfortable in their own skins. Donald isn't one of those people. The rain rains again, harder, stops again. His wet shirt clings at his shoulders when he shrugs inside it. Brush is breaking as a dog charges through the brush. The rain makes it feel like forest instead of woods, like Donald's in something bigger than he's in. Morning bells clamor in a distant steeple. Fallen leaves ride downriver to the dam. Most people are many people. Donald is only Donald. Exposed tree roots. Sodden little hollows. At each bend along the path he doesn't run into anybody. My shirt is wrong, he's thinking. Then up ahead: Somebody walking. Somebody else.

You Don't Have To

You don't have to keep going down to the river, you know. It's not always a pleasant place. Bears were sighted there recently. Spring floods have uprooted so many trees. Don't forget the strange man with a dog. He was soaking wet, the man. Was he talking to himself? You shouldn't be running away like that. Personally, I think with all this rain, the ground is hurt. It's doing things that won't support us, falling away in places. You're going to put your foot down one evening without looking and the ground won't be there. Is this what you want? You'll be tumbling down deep into a hole, asking yourself over and over, Well, Well?

Roger That

I left home with a camera early that day. There was no occasion. I just knew I had no idea what I'd miss if I were not where something interesting might happen. In Tarrytown, nobody ever went home. The folk bathed by the riverside. I found some empty railroad tracks for perspective. I found an old gas pump with Pegasus flying, and some rusting leaves. Down a dirt road in summer a farmer wandered toward the vanishing point. Howdy, old farmer, I said. So long, he said. And night soft fell upon Tarrytown.

Wood Came Down the River

Wood came down the river and a house was built of it, a house by the river. A house of driftwood is opposed to its nature. Unlike driftwood, houses prefer to stay put. Houses set up house in a place where it is conceived that a house should be. But with driftwood one can never be sure. In a house of driftwood one lives among old departed currents that made the wood what it came to be. The drift though that held the wood together can always return to lead the wood away, the helpless wood.

Night Table

Linda has two sons in college. She walks down to the river every night with a friend. Linda tells her friend about furniture Linda wants to give away, a dresser and a footstool, a night table and a rug. Linda's house has acquired an echo, a voice that answers her voice. Linda's friend listens to Linda, listens and listens, as Linda and Linda's friend walk down by the river, the river at night. Linda knows her friend is there in the dark, she can hear her listening. Something up ahead breaks free through the brush and slinks across the path. Fisher cat, says Linda to her friend.

Weightless

Balls sat in the air at once, weightless above the juggler. The juggler's hands were free. The balls were planets and the juggler was unemployed. He was standing near the river after school was out. No one passing by. The balls in the air were a theory of gravity, the birth of a solar system. Smoke sank through the trees, smoke with no source, a nebula of smoke. It was the season of burning leaves, and the World Series. Time to replace smoke detector batteries. The juggler knew a hermit on a mountaintop with a radio. The hermit had terrific reception. He got the games. He got messages in languages he couldn't decipher, messages from other planets. No interference.

Lucy Lost a Glove

Lucy lost a glove along the river. She had acorns in her pocket and a ticket for a show. There were four or five ducks watching her. With her bare hand she picked up another acorn, the cap tilted a little on top like a beret. Lucy understood that the word Lucy had something to do with dawn. The ducks pretended to ignore her. Some tattered snowflakes had located her glove in a corner where she would be unlikely to find it.

A Box of Records

Someone placed a box of records by the curb because it was hoped that someone would want to take them away. They're records no one wants but maybe someone will want them. Someone driving will stop. Someone walking will stop. That is the pleasure of looking through records. Then the sun clears the tree across the street and shines on the records and makes the colors of the record jackets festive even as it robs them of their pigments. Someone will stop and rescue them from the sun. Someone will look up at the empty house behind the box of records at the curb to see if someone is watching. The people on the jackets smile and smile with their best hair, maintaining resolve all night in a box by the curb. Someone will stop and bring them home and listen to what they have to sing. Someone will carry them off out of the rain. Someone will spread them on the grass to dry.

Up Ahead

Up ahead a young man is walking, and up ahead of him, a dog. The man's jacket is the color of the leaves falling around him. I'm walking slower so I won't catch up. He throws a stick for the dog and the dog brings it back. The dog won't let go of the stick and then the dog lets go of the stick. The man throws the stick again. Again the dog goes running. To the left, the river is catching falling leaves. Beds of wet leaves are fermenting on the ground. Another dog comes charging out of the woods to the right and barrels at the first dog. The two of them run off shoulder to shoulder, crashing into each other. A woman who's just stepped from the woods joins the man. He starts walking slower. It's not a long path, really. It's not much longer than a short path.

Silent River

A door opened from under a pile of leaves near the river and two convicts climbed out. They used their caps to dust off their pant legs. They brushed each other's backs. One of the convicts brought two cigarettes from the bib of his overalls. The other one produced a match. They sat on a log. A jogger approached and stopped near them, bending over to catch his breath. But the jogger didn't see the two convicts, just a pair of tree stumps and a halo of mist. Then two women came along. A dog was running in circles ahead of them, running and chasing its tail. They dallied to admire the two convicts who looked like a vegetable garden in early summer. Then a newspaper delivery boy with a canvas bag loaded with news rolled to a halt at the feet of the two convicts. He saw only brush. So he took the canvas bag from his shoulder and heaved it behind the brush since who reads newspapers anyway. The convicts recognized they'd come to the right spot and saw no reason to move on, so they smoked some more. It became night. Then the northern lights appeared above the river, but a very small version of the northern lights, five inches long. The two convicts were moved at last to speak. The northern lights hovers greenly in place tonight like a luna moth on a thread, said one of the convicts. Nope, said the other convict, it drapes like Marie Curie's luminous handkerchief. Nope, said the first convict, it looks like a fluorescent dishrag after a party in Vermont. Nope, said the second one, it looks like curtains for an Irish mouse. Nope, said the first one, that's not it either. I guess not, the second convict said, scratching something in the dirt.

Radio Midnight

—for Jack

The night bird has one song that just goes on ahead, without fin-
ish. All night one spare tune resists melody. When it moves us,
we think it's moving us forward, across an open plain. Think of
the road that way, like the next hour, there because we're on it.
What's out front falls away, black ribbon. We more or less go
along with it, against our wills, cheerfully uneasy. More more
than less.

Inside the Hollow

Snow turned everything to snow. One after another, children made their way into the snow to find where it is the snow ends. Houses dotting the hill stayed dark. Wind was picking up and arranging shreds of loose snow. The children spread across the countryside. The last child, following no footprints, heard something under the wind and walked in that direction. As she wandered west, the sound brightened and became music, a little band of brass and strings under a roof somewhere, the kind of music people listen to on blankets while eating food they made at home, a ferry docked nearby with strings of lanterns and news from the mainland. She came to where the music sounded most brightly, a blue hollow the size of a bowl scooped out of a snow bank, its walls resonating as the last of the sky darkened. Inside the hollow, a small black-suited conductor kept his back to her, thrusting his arm at the cornets. A pleasant well-heeled crowd had settled in for the evening. One place, though, between some blankets, was open down front, so she stepped closer to the bandstand. The ferry tethered to the dock rocked and bumped against tires fixed to the pylons. Down the gangplank, tourists walked rented bicycles under swinging strands of lights.

Biography of My Clothes

—for Nik

On my other shirt geese are startled out of the rushes. And on the back of the shirt is the name of a bowling team, a bowling team from Michigan. When I bought the shirt I was in transit, in Buffalo, and the shirt was in transit too, from Lansing. My other socks are practically new so I wear them less, to keep them new—deep-space socks, black, with comets and planets. My other other socks are Amelia Earhart socks, a portrait of her in goggles on each sock, and a little biography wearing thin. My other pants are corduroy the color of cigarette ash. The musical ridges on them have not yet worn down. They sound like my fifth-grade corduroys, but those were favorites and tight, and after they disappeared I remember no other pants distinctly. There were pants with paint smeared on them that were not pants at all. They were coveralls. What's nice about coveralls is crawling under things. They force one to balance always the distinction between coveralls and overalls. My other jacket is out of sight a long time in the back of the closet. When I see it again, a season away, it will look newer, not as worn as I thought, and I will try it on and think it's not so bad, like what a friend offers when there's a chill in the air. My other shoes are another story. My other shoes believe there are no other shoes. They think I never leave the house. There is no patience like the patience of my other shoes.

Pep Rally

There was a pep rally in the distance. Russia was in the distance, and Arizona. Robert drove into the distance, crossing the desert in an old car, remembering children and falling leaves for effect. Robert spent his life in movies. He was acting in a movie even now, as he drove a convertible, the camera overhead and trailing him slightly, now the camera coming in for a side-shot. Robert was heading to a place where they call him Bob. There's a Bob in the distance, Robert thought. The camera kept watching him for hints. There's an amusement park in the distance, Robert thought, though his look said something about destiny, a hard look he made for the camera to make the camera think he was thinking more than he was. The Devil's Frying Pan, Robert thought. If Robert thought about falling leaves, he was constructing rue for the camera. If Robert thought about children they made him a wistful Robert for the camera. It made him look like he was thinking about Agnes in the future, which is also the distance, Agnes and a bowl of grapes.

Chisholm Trail

Lucy located the Chisholm Trail on a map. When she thought of the Chisholm Trail, she pictured the Mohawk Trail, since it was the only trail she'd actually traveled. But the Mohawk is a road not a trail: souvenir shops selling moccasins and corncob pipes, and a gas station she bought a tire tube from, and a lookout tower from where the peaks of two states were visible. It was sunny along the Mohawk Trail and possible to see everything. A truck driver was drinking coffee from a styrofoam cup. A robin was yanking a worm from the grass. A mother and daughter couldn't decide on which postcards to buy—the one of rushing spring waters, or the one of the shop where they were standing now, through a window of which, in the postcard, snow could be seen falling. The road was gone. A small group of Mohawks was hunting near a stream, a path they often used that went west and then turned a little.

Kindest Man

I leave the drugstore with a bag of purchases. On the sidewalk I see Hans, who I haven't seen in years. But I stop myself from saying his name. He's very tall like Hans, with bushy eyebrows. Hans though doesn't have a red beard nor have I ever seen him in a black leather coat. I close my mouth before a greeting comes out, and pass by, lugging my purchases. The last time I saw Hans he was still in middle management. He'd got a promotion—did I hear that right? Another step up the ladder, or was he selling ladders? I've never seen Hans in a hardware store, a realization that haunts me still. I turn the corner, lost in thought about Hans, when who should I see but Hans. It's been so long. I want to tell Hans about what I've seen, and congratulate him too, if I'm right, about the promotion. This time though it's a much shorter Hans, a Hans I could imagine from a family of tumblers, wiry and compact, with a trim black moustache. Oh Hans, I think, you really have changed careers but I say nothing because the man who could be Hans now turns to say a word to an even more compact man to his right, another man who could be Hans, if Hans were even more compact and wiry, a man with an even blacker moustache. Two Hanses, I'm thinking, look what time has done. How the years have gone by, I'm thinking, since I've spoken with Hans and now it's at least twice today that I've almost seen him, it's at least twice that he's fooled me. Hans wouldn't stoop to trickery. Hans is the kindest man I've ever known. He's a birder. He keeps dead birds in the freezer and studies them. Birders are a kind, elusive people, easily spooked. I grip my bag of purchases in my other hand since my first hand is tired. When did I last have coffee with Hans? Was it a rare moment when our families didn't need us, when our businesses were secure? It was in a different city, I think, we ran into each other in a train station, we drank coffee and chatted, he was going one way and I was going the other. It seemed then that so much time wouldn't go by that we wouldn't do everything we said we'd do. Then in the very moment that I despair of not seeing Hans, I see Hans. It's been so long I almost don't recognize him. But there he is. In overalls smeared with grease, he's hooking up a parked car to the back of a tow-truck. He's perhaps the largest Hans I could ever imagine. His weight has taken him over and made him like several Hanses. Is this the direction his career path took? I want to tell Hans all about the kinds of thoughts I've been having lately. But Hans is smoking a cigar, a black, wet-looking thing. The years have not been kind. Hans looks like he's taken it on the chin. But who am I to talk? Who after all these years would recognize me either? I decide not to say anything. I keep walking. If this is what the years have had in store for us, I don't want to know any more. It's a small town though and I can't hope to get away from it. I suspect I will continue to see Hans wherever I go. We have history.

Went Down to the River

We went down to the river and we were afraid. We didn't know what would happen if we went down to the river. We didn't know if anyone would see us go down to the river or if we'd see anyone. We didn't bring supplies. We didn't bring a phone. We wanted to see what the damage was and we were afraid of what the damage was. We were afraid the damage might lift us up and take us with it. We were afraid of what damage we might become. Everywhere was caught in the drift. Currents had become impatient with the river. They were bending it away from what it was, toward where we were standing. The town had already passed down the river, the hotel and the mill, a girl asleep on a mattress. The story had been told about the river but there was other damage yet to be done. Then we saw somebody come down to the river. Somebody else had come to find what we had found.

Shrunken Tools

He was handed down a collection of shrunken tools. There was a claw hammer and a ball-peen hammer, box wrenches and open-end wrenches and ratchets, needle-nose pliers, vise-grips, screwdrivers of assorted shapes—Phillips and slot—with dark wooden handles. There was a plane, a set of files, a device calibrated to measure down to a thousandth of a millimeter. There was a crow bar, a lug wrench, a hacksaw, awls and punches, wire brushes, clamps and wedges. The tools were clean and cared-for, none larger than a paper match, bundled in strips of chamois, and stored in a sturdy metal chest the size of a small band-aid box, mysteriously useless. The box gave a pleasing weight in his hand, but it seemed as though he was gazing through a keyhole into an ancient room, with nothing inside it the right size to fix.

Henry

If we hadn't screwed our hats down tight on our heads, where would those hats have gone—flying up into the air at once, a flock of hats, like starlings, a black acrobatic cloud bending and diving, like starlings we saw one October at the beach, a rubbery swarm swooping and morphing, and one of us unleashed the big white greyhound, and he bolted as if right out of the gate, sand exploding around us, Henry racing away until he was no more than a white speck down the shore, part of the horizon, like a tiny crazy gull.

Bad News

Bad news was coming in the mail. Vita opened an envelope expecting bad news, but while it wasn't good news, the news was not bad. Nevertheless, she walked away from the pile of new mail, leaving the rest unopened. She put a light on because it had gotten dark in the house, like Monday in a museum. The next day felt like some bad news had come but it was only Tuesday. She went to the store and forgot what to buy. On the way out, she held the door to the market open for an old lady, and then held the door longer as a family from out of town arrived in need of directions. In the mail the following day the news was not bad, and that was bad news, if what was expected was bad news, but not the worst news. The real bad news was that bad news was on its way. At best, the bad news was waylaid, pending sorting in a distant processing center, possibly St Louis, one of the finest sorting hubs of its kind for first class mail, not to mention small packages, and bulk.

A Request

The river put in a request that nobody write about it that day. After a long spell of neglect, the river was getting tons of press: men without raincoats, boys with matches, women running dogs. The river was not in charge of its clichés. The river was a victim too, a victim of location. Not one morning passed, when the river, lying in bed, didn't think of packing it in. There'd be headlines: River on the Run. But the only bad press is no press. Death to the pathetic fallacy, thought the river. Something, said the river out loud, something something.

Things in the Cellar

He wanted to go down to the cellar but it wasn't allowed. He had business down there he wouldn't explain but it was clear he couldn't manage the stairs. There were things in the cellar he needed to be among: tools, tuna in cans. There was a steel rod that needed straightening. A bear had bent it outside going after the birdseed that had filled the pan suspended from the rod. Animals were arriving in the backyard to eat. Small ones were nesting under the eaves. The animals were hungry and wanted something. They rummaged at night, figuring out the locks. In the afternoons they appeared disguised in the backyard, reading the meter, collecting fallen limbs, as if they had real home lives. A coyote in a zoot suit showed up often near sundown, a coyote with credentials, who'd take stairs two at a time if it had the chance. In the cellar a man could find strength—a good place to remember, and dark.

Lucy Declines

Lucy declines to save her place. She's saved her place in so many other books that she can no longer choose which way to go. The places she's saved look worthy and out of context, trains of thought that left the station. What was she leaving that she thought she should return to? *He moved back out to the desert—The plane was half empty—But would not this greatly add to the worries—The winter that now comes with light and height—* A field covered in snow is pressed with dog prints among which Lucy can find no pattern.

What Then

What then if it was Friday, in the afternoon, the clouds had parted, the roads were opened, and the winds were picking up. What then if there was no river, everyone at the moment not there, not one of them showing up. Things carry on by themselves and become other things. A piano tuner far off elsewhere was packing up his tuning tools. He had perfect pitch, and made adjustments to every tone he heard, mental calibrations, averting his face. A handier man may you never see. The piano tuner strapped his tuning kit to the carrier on the back of his bike. He was apt to take the path where the river goes, the river that invents its moment as he rolls along it, the river making and holding itself like a tone, decaying after he has passed, as he turns not around. What then if it wasn't Friday, the roads were cleared, and the winds were packing up. What then if there was the river, where everyone had left it, had left it on its own, and what came next came next, and the windows being windows were raised.

How Are Things in Your Town

A scrap of wind drags a leaf down the sidewalk after midnight. Now the leaf changes direction like a window shopper. A mannequin presses a hand against the shop window, lips parted. It's a fine thing to be helped, to climb a ladder during a full moon. A car without a muffler takes another pass on Main Street, pigeons half-asleep. There is no Leap Day this year. Clearly someone knows someone.

Chronicle Forsworn

There are days so clear I can see what I want. I can see towns in Connecticut. I can see too at times how little there is to see and then I must rely on other tools. There is a field that I return to, a meeting at noon, after that, the rest of Friday. Then there's a lack of evidence, and who makes up what's made-up, a lonely shipping clerk in a small bright office right now checking squares on an inventory template, glancing at a watch. Packages all at once are lifting off the ground, circling above vast cities; the terrain tips first one way and then the other, as contents shift. And how weather overlooks the town common, like a clock tower.

Hat with Flaps

It was a hat I could never get out from under. I lost it over and over. Somehow it always came back. I had a nice navy blue pea cap that was borrowed years ago. Since then I've been given replacement caps but none have ever sat on my head the right way. Now I go without a cap. In the mudroom a stack of hats sits on a shelf, like a painting of a shelf with hats in it. The hats are wearing hats. There's an old straw Stetson I wear to ballgames. I bought it in a haberdashery on Nantucket. Or in a gas station in Pensacola. Anyway, sea birds were flying. On Friday afternoons, we push back our hats. My old straw Stetson has a few raggedy finger-sized holes in it along the crown. Sticking a finger in one of the holes feels like a finger trap. The holes are like holes in the thatched roof of a beach cottage I've never visited. Among the other hats is a costume hat. It looks like Sam Spade's fedora. It never loses its shape so it always looks like a perfect hat, except that it can never be worn as a hat.

Fraught with Sudden Appearances

Pete's dog sat behind the window and watched the air outside where Pete once stood. Pete's dog was troubled that a man who could occupy air the way Pete does can vanish the next minute and not return for possibly years. It was only one of the many miracles of Pete. Pete's slippers were a miracle of comfort. The records Pete played made Pete pivot, like a dog, or made him stand still, staring into space, as if Pete too were waiting for Pete to come home. Pete required close scrutiny. He possessed a miraculous control of food. At any moment something wonderful could appear in Pete's hand. The magic of Pete was its own reward. Outside the window, the world was fraught with sudden appearances and disappearances, and into it Pete stepped fearlessly every day. Every day Pete would find a curtain in the air and step behind it and there was no more Pete. The air was a cruel master. Pete's dog could summon Pete by assembling the clothes Pete left behind. It always worked. Upon Pete's glad return Pete would gather up the assembled Pete and put its pieces away. It was important always to listen to the sounds Pete made that Pete's dog couldn't decipher. And the sounds Pete didn't make, they meant something too, and the sound of keys, the door opening. The air abounded with clues, the kingdom of Pete's air, through which the one known as Pete comes and goes.

Imaginary Americans

The river started going the other way. It remembered something it had once been told. It dragged mill bricks back upstream from the 1874 dam-burst. Blunt glacial rocks tumbled in reverse. Fallen trees stood up. Imaginary Americans spectated from the banks. The river narrowed by pride. Clouds and floaters never hold still. News is what surprises us. I wonder how many pick-up trucks I'll see on the road when I'm significantly older.

In the Desert

We visited him in the desert. And what we'd found was true. In a fit of profound irritation he'd dispensed with worldly possessions, all but the mule. A path was formed under his feet in the shape of a large donut upon which the mule followed. Saying donut was our small portion of ridicule, so completely had he acclimated to life without us. He needed nobody. Still, we made dust to visit him, and our dust commingled with his dust, and the commingled dust formed a ragged body from which we thought it was possible that a miracle could emerge. The mule was the one true skeptic, how it slathered along, head bobbing privately, not to confirm or deny. Nevertheless, at the appointed time, arrived a pilgrim, who fell to his knees, and without hands, prayed for hands that he might pray.

One of the Great Bobs

Robert was going to the movies. He was going to see a movie with Bob in it, one of the great Bobs. One of the great Bobs appearing on the big screen would create the impact of an epic Bob, the kind of Bob someone like Robert could see from far away. It had not been a big day for Robert but he was fine with knowing that, since he expected nothing large of the day. It had actually been a small day for Robert, among his smallest, possibly one of the smallest days for anyone, ever, ever since the very first day when such measurements were first taken. Robert could see men coming with tape measures and graphs, in black coats and black trousers and black hats, how they in their indefinite number were in themselves actually quite small and indistinct from one another but nevertheless endowed with a certain stature by the task they performed. As they set about their business, the business of scale, Robert left for the movies. He saw in the mirror himself as he drove down the freeway, his eye inhabiting one corner of the mirror, and mountains in the distance and homes in the mountains where at least one of the great Bobs must live, and the road behind him unspooling back into what would have been a sunrise, if it were a different time of the day.

Ducks

Reading had become, for him, like counting ducks on a pond. Words kept flying away, or dipping into the water, or hiding behind one another. Mysterious formations elevated themselves, changing shape in the widening sky, unlike ducks.

On the Other Hand

Ducks on the other hand had become remnants of vaudeville. They squawked about soup, about weather, about who was in town that weekend, about wives. I sat and watched them each day because they needed an audience and there was almost no audience left. They were emissaries from Grandfather's youth. They kept the music halls open, even after the music halls had closed.

The River So Often

Eventually she went to the river so often that there were times that it wasn't a river. It became a thing with no name or with a name that is used for a different thing. Anvil, oxbow, crag. It disappeared behind the name it was given. Or when it bore no name, it was gone all the way. Then she could stand there and not know where she was, which wasn't pleasant, necessarily, but not unpleasant, to stand before the familiar and find it drained of explanation. It could even be a relief to be suspended so, the fact of the matter not a matter of fact.

Small Clearing

There was a small clearing near a bend in the river. I'd pause there from time to time while out on a walk, after the kids had grown. It seemed like a good place to stop and think, perfect void among the trees. The mind would go happily blank. Then one day, ashes appeared in the clearing, and a few beer cans. The next day I saw more ashes, a few large rocks. Rocks for sitting, I feared. Then a log appeared, and drag marks in the sand the log had left behind. Next day, a handkerchief someone had knotted around a low-hanging limb marked the spot. I knew what was coming. After a week, another log showed up, empty spaghetti cans, a rumpled sleeping bag. It was simple arithmetic now. I turned and headed for home. Up ahead a dog barked in the cold shallows, a strange dog I'd never see again.

Students Moved Around a Lot

Students moved around a lot before settling in. They saw congruencies everywhere, kinships like crows on a wire. There was a physics teacher too who gave the appearance of being always unsettled. The students couldn't help notice he was often late—the tails of his raincoat flying behind him as he ran down the hall, ancient exams spilling from a briefcase too stuffed to close. Maybe his wife hated the northeast, or maybe, for him, physics was a disappointment. He looked incomplete. And even though he'd promise otherwise, he failed to grade tests or homework on time. Therefore, the students, at sea, never knew what they knew and what they didn't know. They showed up unsettled, in dress, in halting speech patterns. That's years ago now. Yet it feels like yesterday, or even today. Here they are coming through the doors of the ancestral home. Mother is baking. Tomorrow is, of all days, Thanksgiving.

Wrote That Down

Each time he started to write something, he thought it was him-self writing it, this is it, he thought, this sounds like him there-fore it must be him writing it, it must be what it sounds like to be like him, to be himself writing it, this thought, words in a par-ticular kind of order on a particular kind of paper, a mind ad-dressing itself, See here, his mind said to itself, addressing itself, so he wrote that down, and looked then out the window, where, near the street, stood a half-bare tree that he could see only part of, and down the street, where he could only imagine, ran the river he couldn't see at all, into which yellow and orange leaves were falling, and he wrote that down, and at just that moment crossing her lawn was the woman who lives across the street, who is pleasing to look at, especially from far away, perfectly fine close up, but even more pleasing from far away.

Arthur's Television

Arthur was watching television. The people in the television were working very hard to make Arthur react to them. One person in the television said something to another person in the television then waited for Arthur's reaction. Then the other person in the television said something back. The other person then also waited for Arthur's reaction, anticipating possibly an even stronger reaction. Then the first person said something again to the other person, and waited, and according to the math, expected Arthur to provide them with his strongest reaction yet. Finally a third person, the capper, entered the television. The third person in the television said nothing at all. The simple appearance of the third person in the television was supposed to be enough to induce one of the strongest reactions possible from Arthur. But Arthur just sat in his chair watching them. What a day. He had nothing left to give to the people in the television. So the people in the television, undaunted, tried another set-up, but this time they added a chimpanzee. Arthur sat and sat. The people in the television studied Arthur a moment. They were not easily discouraged. This time they kept the chimp and added a very messy food to the floor. One of them would step in the mess and fall and hurt his back, because an injury to the back is what should provoke the most uncontrollable reaction of all from Arthur. The people in the television performed gamely, if a little desperately. Arthur however provided not even the mildest of reactions. He could not make room in his heart for the people in the television. At last the people in the television stopped the show. Two of the people and the chimp helped the third person—who really had hurt his back—get up to his feet. They stood around with their hands in their pockets and gazed searchingly into Arthur's face. Then the people in the television shrugged and picked up their things and walked out of the television and the chimp followed closely behind them. Arthur sat staring into empty rooms in the television. Something lodged there was appealing to him—the clean lines, the artificial sunlight entering stage left. Then a new person entered the television, with a jacket hooked on his fingers and slung over his shoulder. Arthur thought this must be the sponsor. As the new person in the television came into focus Arthur looked closer, and recognized it was his dad, but it was his dad as a much younger man. His dad's hair was dark and thick and parted carelessly on the side. Arthur's dad was gently smiling. It's a trap, said Arthur. I know it. Arthur's dad continued smiling gently. Looking right at Arthur from inside the television, he began saying something, but Arthur couldn't hear him. He must be on mute, said Arthur. Arthur leaned forward and turned up the volume control. But even though Arthur's dad went on speaking Arthur could hear nothing. Arthur turned it up full blast. Still nothing. His dad seemed to be genially repeating a question, wanting something. It's a trap, said Arthur, standing up. Arthur was following the mouth of his dad. I can't read lips, said Arthur. He's nice now but wait till after we break for station identification.

River River

River of rain sluicing down the street, river of storm drain and debris, river of rain meets river, obvious river, river within river, furtive river, river fed by rivers, river churning river, river unmaking its bed, river of oxbow and break, river of how river goes, river of no rivers, river gone and gone, river of former glories, river gone to party, reluctant river, river shy in groups, river with dumb smile, river of too much to drink, river heaving in bushes, river weaving home deadheading mailboxes, river nostalgic near end of summer, river of bad hearing, river of nod

Industrial Film

Robert gave to the movies and the movies gave to Robert. He was thinking about industrial films, and filmy sunlight filtered through clouds along the horizon, great big pink slabs of clouds beyond where the road goes, industrial clouds, layers of industry, big industry of the West. Possibility, he said, addressing a big room of big wheels, wide open, limitless. Big clouds, he said, big dreams, big shoes to fill. This big makes a person big. Mountain echoes, he said, atmospheric chemical transfers, big buses of next big things, big hats. Unbridled brides, he said, remote settings. Cavernous interiors so cavernous one's voice just goes and goes and goes, said Robert's voice, launching into the ozone like one of the earliest satellites.

To the Editor

With the holidays here, I wonder where everyone has gone. The mailman brought packages this morning but returned to take them back, since he was mistaken. They'd actually been addressed to a similar residence in a kindred neighborhood. He seemed to suspect me of something but obviously it wasn't my fault. Maybe it wasn't that obvious. I fear in these moments I'm the only one here who understands what's going on, so where does that leave us? To say us is discomforting, particularly when I'm the one standing on the porch, and the mail truck's hauling away things that weren't meant for me. I feel moved to address this, to talk about us, and the outrages that daily we face, that there must be an explanation for why this is happening now, all at once, and why it never happened in our youth, when we bowed our heads before the onslaught of civilities, and said, You're welcome.

Subject to Scrutiny

Snow remains on the north side of the roof. The north side of the roof is what I see. I think of the south side of the roof when I see the north side. The south side of the roof must have no snow. The south side must be warm. The south side must be warm especially in the afternoon. I'm reminded of lizards sunning on rocks. The rocks are as warm as roofs in the afternoon. The lizards don't move all day long. Roofs are like islands without people. Darwin studies lizards through a spyglass. Darwin approaches in a small boat. Though small the small boat is heavy. Old wood on the high seas is heavy yet buoyant. Darwin's brow juts out like a ledge. Darwin's brow is like an eave on which the snow remains.

Dollar Bill

I found a dollar bill while walking the path along the river. I almost didn't see it. It was the color of moss, peeking out from under some leaves. As I wiped the bill on my pants to clean it, I scanned around for more. On a rock sat a paper coffee cup with an inch or two of rainwater in it, and at the bottom of the cup, two quarters, three nickels, and a dime. I drained the rainwater through my fingers, catching the coins, and wondered if someone was saving them and would return shortly. So I put the coins in my pocket and kept moving. Just ahead on the path I found another dollar bill, folded and pressed into the dirt. I picked up the bill, pinching it between finger and thumb, and shook off the clotted soil. Unfolding it, I found another dollar bill folded inside that one, and folded inside that, a five-dollar bill, and inside that, a twenty. It was becoming too much. Scattered around were other bills. I looked back to see if anyone was seeing me, if anyone was coming, and examined the path, reaching down and picking up, searching the ground cover beyond, leaf-by-leaf, inching further and further into the woods. With enough money, I speculated, one day, I'd buy a clarinet.

With a Broken Arm in a Rowboat

The man with a broken arm in a rowboat hears music coming from the beach. The music has sand in it, and soda bottles howling in a steady breeze, and seagulls ripping open a potato chip bag. It's Friday evening at the beach and the sun's gone and so are the people. Little waves nudge up against a crumbling sea wall and make a watery kind of static like the gap between two radio signals. On and on floats the man with the broken arm, his one good arm pulling his one good oar.

A Good Run

When I stood by the side of the road, I was hungry, and I stuck out a thumb, and my ride gave me a peach. When I stood again, I wasn't thinking about anything, so I stuck out my thumb and a stranger drove me for a hundred miles and gave me some of the money he had stolen from someone else. When I stood by the side of the road, I was in Colorado, where I didn't have to stick out my thumb, and I stood there forever reading a paperback. When I stood forever by the side of the road, I didn't have to stand there any longer than that, and the next thing I drank a beer on the back of a flat-bed and that didn't last long enough. When I stood by the side of the road, I was in a city I'd never been in before, and the bus schedule made no sense, and I was too shy to ask directions, so I walked with my thumb out, and walked some more. When I stood by the side of the road, I didn't know how I got there, it was a tiny northern town with one school bus, and I thought I'd come back there some day. When I stood for less than a minute, that was all the time it took, and the wind in the convertible made my hair stand up. When I stood by the side of the road, I thought of other rides, and the first raindrop hit me, an unusually large generous raindrop.

Clouds Shifting

I went down to the river and thought. A dog ran by. Then a woman passed listening to a cell phone. Clouds were shifting in a big meaningful way but she didn't seem to notice. It was only I who noticed—I and my thought among the rocks. My thought shifted in a big meaningful way, like a parking officer opening his ticket pad. The simile was inappropriate but it was too late. I was committed to the relationship. The old mental hospital grounds across the river were becoming a mixed-income community, with speed bumps and articulated buses. Things were progressing nicely. Another dog ran by and marveled at my incapacity for closure. I picked up someone's missing glove and hung it from a low branch where it could easily be found. There were several ways to leave the path and I would keep walking until one presented itself.

Wolf's at the Door

Spring-cleaning comes late in the year. We never expect it to but there it is. Wolf's at the door, says Harold. We head upstairs and have a look-see for what can go. Harold says let's get this old couch out of here. It's hard to imagine that couch without him on it but never mind. We drag it out to the curb. With luck, before nightfall, someone will take it away. Harold flops down for one last sit. In my mind, it's complete. A black squirrel clatters through the branches. Great, says Harold, here come the acorns.

Acknowledgments

Thanks to the editors of the following journals:

32 Poems, Big Big Wednesday, Burnside Review, Conduit, Fell Swoop, FIELD, Gettysburg Review, Green Mountains Review, jubilat, Massachusetts Review, New Ohio Review, Salt Hill Journal, Verse Daily.

Several of these pieces appeared in the chapbook, *An Unpleasant Sense of Being Frank* (Fell Swoop #141).

And with gratitude always to Alexandra Kennedy, Dara Wier, William Waltz, and Joel XJ Dailey.

The FIELD Poetry Series